Ten Easy Tips for Staying Safe

Cindy James

The Rosen Publishing Group's

READING ROOM
Collection™

New York

Published in 2002 by The Rosen Publishing Group, Inc.
29 East 21st Street, New York, NY 10010

First Library Edition 2002

Book Design: Ron A. Churley

Photo Credits: Cover, p. 1 © Len Rubenstein/Index Stock; p. 4 © Mitch Diamond/Index Stock; pp. 7, 8, 12, 16, 19 © Donna Scholl; p. 11 © Kevin Beebe/Index Stock; p. 15 © Myrleen Cate/Index Stock; p. 20 © Craig Witkowski/Index Stock.

Library of Congress Cataloging-in-Publication Data

James, Cindy, 1973-
  Ten easy tips for staying safe / Cindy James.
    p. cm. — (The Rosen Publishing Group's reading room collection)
Includes index.
  ISBN 0-8239-3721-6 (library binding)
  1. Safety education—Juvenile literature. 2. Children and
strangers—Juvenile literature. 3. Children—Crimes
against—Prevention—Juvenile literature. [1. Safety.] I. Title. II.
Series.
  HQ770.7 .J36 2002
  613.6—dc21
                                        2001007028

Manufactured in the United States of America

For More Information
McGruff.org
http://www.mcgruff.org/

Stay Alert, Stay Safe
http://www.sass.ca/kmenu.htm

Contents

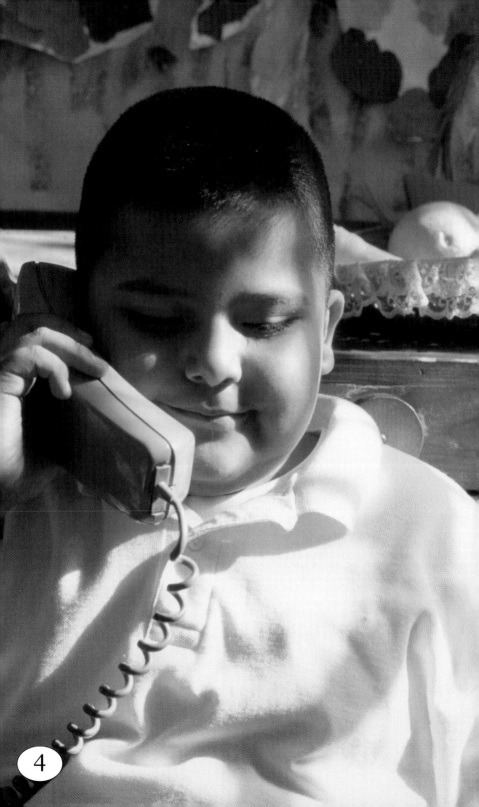

4

Tip 1
Dial 911 for Help

Most of the people around us are nice, but some people aren't so nice. Some people might even want to hurt you. The good news is that there are things you can do to stay safe.

The first step is very easy. Call **911** if you are ever in **trouble**. You can call from home, from someone else's house, or from a pay phone. You never have to pay to call 911.

 Call 911 if you are ever in trouble.

Tip 2
Don't Talk to Strangers

A **stranger** is someone you don't know. You can't tell which strangers are nice just by looking at them. You shouldn't trust a stranger just because he or she has a friendly smile. The smartest thing to do is to not talk to strangers at all. Don't worry about being **rude** by not talking to strangers. A good person will understand why you won't talk.

Get away from a stranger who keeps trying to talk to you.

Tip 3
Don't Be Tricked

What if a stranger drove up next to you and offered you some candy or an ice-cream cone to get into the car with her? What if she said your mom asked her to pick you up? What would you say?

No matter what a stranger offers you or says to you, say no and walk away quickly. Don't be fooled by any of these tricks.

Never accept anything from a stranger, no matter how much you want it.

Tip 4

Don't Panic

If someone ever makes you feel strange or **uncomfortable**, don't panic. Instead, stay **calm** and think first. What's the safest thing for you to do? Is there a police officer nearby? Is there a store where you can go for help? By keeping calm, you are helping yourself to do the safe, smart thing.

Staying calm when something bad happens makes it easier to find the help you need.

Tip 5
Walk with a Buddy

Always walk with a **buddy** when you are going anywhere. If you walk to and from school every day, do the safe thing. Walk with a friend. If there's a day when one of you has to walk alone, make another plan. Ask your mom or dad to drive you to school and pick you up afterward. You and your parents could even walk home together.

Walking with a buddy is the safe thing to do. It is also more fun than walking home alone.

Tip 6
Know Your Names and Numbers

Tip one says that you can call 911, but you should also know your home phone number. If you can, you should also learn the phone numbers for your parents at work. Know both their first and last names. Does your parent have a different last name from yours? You should know that, too. **Memorize** these names and numbers. You can even write them on a card and take them with you wherever you go.

Write important names and phone numbers on a card that you can carry with you.

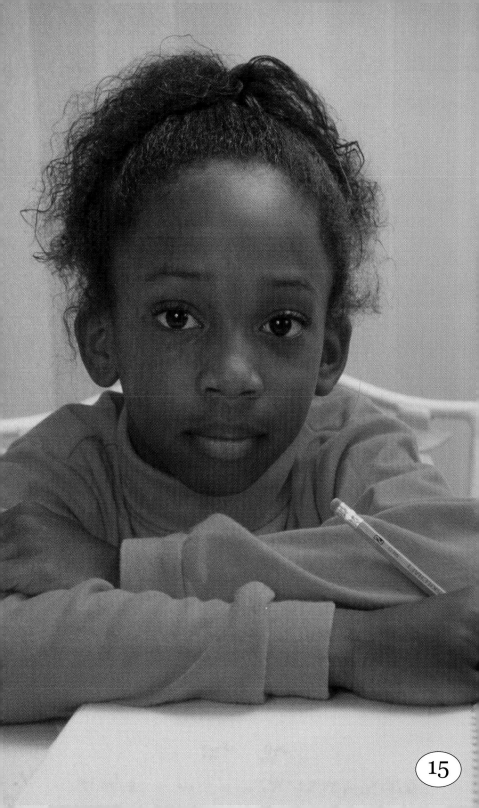

Tip 7
Always Have Emergency Money

You should always carry **emergency** money. You might need money to call your mom or dad on a pay phone to pick you up after school. What if you miss the bus? If it's okay with your parents to take the city bus in an emergency, you will need some money to pay for the trip. Keep the money safe in your backpack or in the pocket of your coat.

Remember: You should only use your emergency money for an emergency.

Tip 8
Know Your
Home-Alone Tips

If you ever have to stay home alone, you and your parent can make a list of things you should do to stay safe. Does your mom want you to open the door for a **neighbor**? Should you answer the phone? Ask your parents for the answers to these questions. You can write them down and put the list where you can find it quickly.

Ask your parents to explain each tip to you as you write them down. Then your tip list will make more sense to you.

Tip 9

Know Your Secret Word

Having a secret word is also a good idea. Only you, your parents, and a person you can trust will know what it is. That way, you know you can trust the person who knows your secret word. If someone tries to pick you up after school and he does not know the secret word, get away from him. Find a safe place where you can call your parents and wait for them to pick you up.

 You and your parent can decide together what your secret word will be. It might help to write it down.

Tip 10
Be Smart

The tenth step to staying safe is to be smart. You've learned some important tips for staying safe wherever you are, but the most important thing is to keep calm. Don't do anything that makes you uncomfortable. If something feels scary or wrong, then it probably is. You can trust your feelings about certain things. Remember: Your safety comes first!

Glossary

buddy A close friend.

calm Quiet and in control.

emergency A sudden need for quick action.

memorize To learn something and be able to remember it when you need to.

neighbor Someone who lives next door to you or nearby.

911 The phone number that is used to get help quickly.

rude Having bad manners; not polite.

stranger Someone you do not know.

trouble A problem, or something that makes you nervous.

uncomfortable Feeling scared and unsure of yourself or something around you.

Index